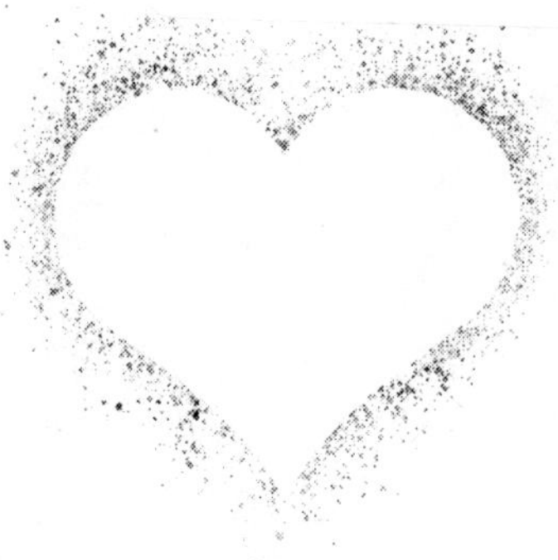

INNER WINNER

FINDING THE GOLD THAT LIES WITHIN

Judy Swallow

INNER WINNER

FINDING THE GOLD THAT LIES WITHIN

Judy Swallow

Golden Brick Road
Publishing House

Inner Winner: Finding the Gold That Lies WIthin

Golden Brick Road Publishing House Inc.

Published in Canada, for Global Distribution by Golden Brick Road Publishing House Inc. www.goldenbrickroad.pub

Interior design by Tara Mixon

For more information email: judy.soulutions@gmail.com

ISBN: trade paperback: 978-1-988736-13-6
ebook: 978-1-988736-14-3

To order additional copies of this book: orders@gbrph.ca

CONTENTS

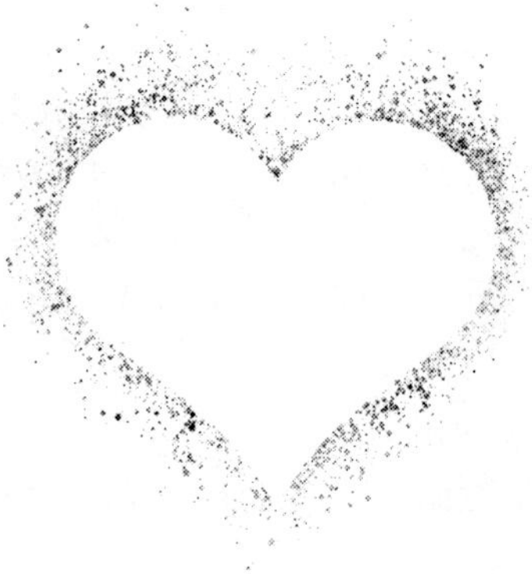

Dedication

To Mom and Dad

Thank you for the perfect imperfections

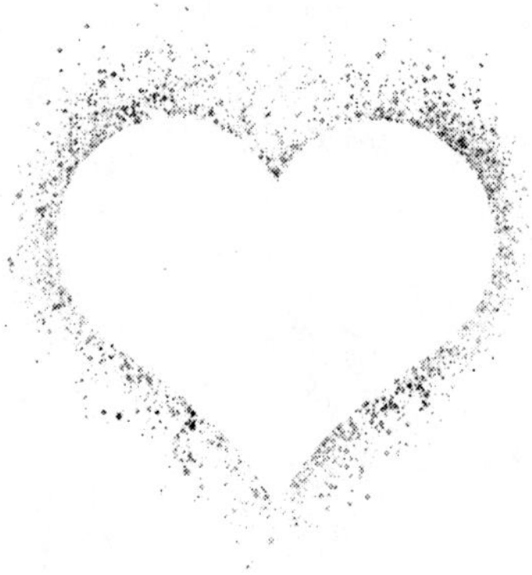

Being An Inner Winner

What does it mean to be an "Inner Winner"?

Not all of us aspire to be Olympic athletes or gold medalists. It is a goal shared by a select few. But I do believe that the desire to win at life is a shared goal. Who wouldn't want to live a life that is in alignment with our deepest dreams and heart felt desires? Just as the athlete needs to train and dedicate time and energy to their endeavor, each of us must do the same to live a life that is the expression of our true self.

Being an Inner Winner is doing whatever it takes to achieve the goal, to challenge and overcome every obstacle on the path. To live authentically and attuned to your highest aspiration takes similar dedication. Ascension in any field requires self-care and love.

"Open your eyes, look within.
Are you satisfied with the life you're living?"
Bob Marley

Self-awareness and introspection can reveal what's hindering the actualization of the best life you imagine for yourself. It is the start of being an Inner Winner. It is the quality of being *soul-y* responsible for yourself and the willingness to do what it takes to achieve the dream.

When I was in my mid-30s and in the second year of the Transpersonal Psychotherapy Training Program,

I had an extraordinary moment where I realized that I am responsible for my life. I wasn't consciously aware that I was blaming others for not living the life I wanted to live. In fact, my *if only* list was long, and something I believed to be right and true: *If only my parents had done this; If only that coach nurtured my talent more; If only people had told me how smart and beautiful I am…I would be more this, that or the other.* I felt justified in feeling that others were responsible for my pain. It's true that they may have contributed to my lack of self-worth, self-love, and self-esteem, but I was the one perpetuating the beliefs.

That is the value in paying attention to your thoughts, feelings, and to your life circumstances as they begin to reveal what is going on beneath the surface of the conscious mind. No one, not my parents, not my teachers, not anyone or anything in my world or environment, past or present, caused my problems. I stopped the blame game, or at least began to. I was truly on the path to soul and sole responsibility for my life.

"You have to grow from the inside out.
None can teach you, none can make you spiritual.
There is no other teacher but your own soul."
Swami Vivekananda

After each moment of enlightenment that I experienced, it was the resulting self-awareness that led me to see what I needed to keep working on and understand in order to further transform my *default setting* of fear to one of faith, faith in myself. The moments of enlightenment, plus the continued persistence and tenacity to gain deeper insights was what led me to cultivate an inner strength to live the life I desired. Inner winning was occurring more and more; I was finding the Gold within: self-value and self-worth that became the foundation on which I stood.

Have you ever noticed that life is always presenting us with the opportunity to see ourselves and what is really going on inside? I am not speaking of when we are doing our day to day—when the world as we know it is comfortable and predictable. I'm talking about those times when we want to stretch our limits, create a dream, challenge our personal status quo—when we need to face our personal truths, whatever they may be, moments when we know that we're living a lie and we choose to acknowledge it or say it doesn't matter: *I will pretend all is fine.* Can you see that these are the times when the qualities of who you truly are, come into play and show how well you are doing at being an Inner Winner, your own champion?

A particular moment I had a few years back, revealed to me how I was really seeing myself. I was watching *The View* on TV. As I was watching it, I began to imagine myself having written a book and being interviewed on the show. For some reason, I was unable to visualize myself speaking clearly, nor could I articulate what the book was about. I was babbling and unclear. I was astounded. Just visualizing this scenario showed me that my self-image surely wasn't one of being an Inner Winner. There was no way I was ready to receive my dreams when I still saw myself as inept.

Yet, what a fabulous moment this turned out to be! Something had changed. I noticed that I didn't feel ashamed that I was still not completely confident. I didn't berate myself; I didn't feel defeated. Like an athlete who has more work to do to get to the top of the podium, I simply had more work and training to do. I had the tools and enough experience to keep chipping away at the fear that was still stopping me from genuinely showing up in my own life and in the world.

When I coach, I do not ask my clients to do something I am not willing to do myself in the vein of overcoming fear, worry or doubt. They have chosen figure skating as their arena and path to learning many life lessons. The challenges of the sport—of achieving the necessary goals, requires them to consistently choose to go beyond their comfort zones. I ask them to have their *Olympic Gold Medal Moment* every step of the way, because they need to make the choice to either be an Inner Winner, or allow the fear and uncertainty to stop them. It's not easy. But what a victory when they challenge the fear and own their truth. I ask them to become aware of their thoughts and self-talk so that they can take their power back and declare what their choice will be. It's one of my most favorite things to teach them—what my spiritual teacher taught me about "monkey mind." In my interpretation and experience "monkey mind," translates to fear, doubt, and worry—all the *what ifs*. It's what I call the FDW highway. Becoming aware of those thoughts, observing their contribution to what I was feeling, and how I was reacting to a situation was so powerful. It reminds me of this quote:

"I've had a lot of worries in my life,
most of which never happened."
Mark Twain

I hold myself accountable to this same process. As a result, I have been able to ascend many personal mountains, and I acknowledge how many *gold medals* I've actually achieved so far. It is so important to take stock of the victories while working on challenges. Step by step, I began all those years ago, and it has brought me here; summiting toward the mountain peak, that up to now is the greatest actualization of my journey from fear, and its many names—into love and all its amazing gifts—the writing of my story and publishing this book.

THE SEEDS ARE PLANTED

As I think back on my childhood years, there are two incidents that stand out. They were small, defining moments that seemed to solidify my life's mission.

The first event occurred when I was standing on the bottom landing of our two story house. My sister was halfway up the stairs and could still see into the living room where our parents were seated. I had no idea what was going on, but she was yelling at them, almost in a rage. I looked up at her, and for a moment, I was totally detached from the situation. I showed no emotion, had no fear. I was simply a spectator. And the more I watched, the more I began to question.

"What makes people tick?"

I was only eight, but I was mesmerized by their interaction, by their *human behavior.*

The second event took place about a year later, while I was walking home from my friend's house. I had cut through the backyard of some other homes to get to my street. As I walked into the driveway, I looked down and saw a large ant crawling, and I was mesmerized by it, by its size. It was so small compared to me.

I have great power over it, I thought.

I went back and forth, debating my options.
I can step on it, or I can let it be.

I decided to *practice my power*, and I stepped on it. I brought my foot down on top of the ant. And when I took it away, I saw the crushed ant and its blood. I was in horror at what I had just done. I am writing this forty-five years later, and the emotion is just as intense. I took that ant's life for no reason. I felt so bad, so guilty. I walked the rest of the way home crying, horrified at what I had done.

In time, my love for psychology started to emerge more prevalently. In fact, I became the first subject of my, *What makes people tick?* exploration. Spirituality also became a huge part of the journey. The ant would eventually teach me that understanding and knowing myself, knowing the power that I AM, is crucial to a life of harmony and a world of love.

A Dream Wants To Be Lived

I have had this dream and passion for so long to help others know of the Gold within, of the inherent power they have to summit any mountain—figuratively or literally. I am grateful beyond words for my journey through the darkness and pain. It has given me the power, wisdom, and the tools that allow me to actualize my *Gold* and do what I know I am here to do: find out what makes people tick by finding out what makes me tick. Through having done this and continuing to do it, I honor the lesson the ant taught me that fateful day; I have power, and I will use it wisely and lovingly. We all have it, and what beauty can be created when we all know within that we are the love we are never without.

Why has it taken so long?

Because I had to honor my truth during the journey. I went to university to get the formal education, to earn a degree; I discovered that it is not the right learning environment for me. I am an experiential learner. University had too much book learning, and that wasn't what I was seeking. I wanted to understand me, my pain, my feeling of not being good enough. There were no answers except one course I took in my third year, Metaphysics in Science and Psychology. I found it! Consciousness is what I was seeking. I got my Bachelor of Arts degree and left the realm of *higher education*. I have loved the School of Hard Knocks and the forms of other private education

I have engaged in. But this tutelage didn't allow for those all-important letters behind my name—the letters that would signify to society that I am able to help others find their truth and live their best life. So, that's what has taken so long. I had to get over what the outside world considers credentials and trust and believe that my humanity is yours too—that I can help others just as I have helped myself.

"Your work is to discover your world and then with all your heart give yourself to it."
Buddha

First Glimpse

Why oh why am I so up and down?
Here and there, not always sound?
I feel good, then I feel bad
So so happy, then oh, so sad.
When I fly, I reach the sky
And here is where I want to remain.
But the call of Life challenges this
It's not always possible to feel this bliss.
The obstacles are always there
And some of them seem so unfair.
How do I rise above all this
To experience true Happiness?
The answer seems so far away
So out of reach for me to attain.

But then I learn the answer is near
The secret to that which I hold so dear.
I turn and look the other way and see within myself
A strength I thought I was without
And is really what it's all about.
Looking within, I do find the wonder of Self-Love
The fantastic, magical power that helps me rise above.
The block that was before me, now just fades away
Exactly like the dark of the dawning new day.
And with this Love, I do overcome
And see that anything can be done.

This is the first poem I wrote after I began my inward journey. I had been reading self-help and spiritual books— getting a first glimpse of the struggle between my ego and soul, between living in fear and living in love. I say *glimpse,* because the journey had just begun, even though I held the hope of maintaining a conscious connection to the truth, love, and power I felt when writing the poem and learning that the answer was near.

At that point, I had the personal experience of knowing there was a way out of my pain and darkness, and this was enough to keep me continually on my quest to live and find the true joy I was dying for.

Dying I was, though I didn't exactly know that. Out of the old, into the new. A long, slow, and at times, anguishing death of my sense of self—who I thought I was, and what I thought life was.

I thank God for this death.

These poems are all, in essence, a portrait of my climb up the mountain of life.

THE I OF THE HURRICANE

Whirling winds within me rage
Threatening to upset my tailored stage.
The confusion and sadness I tried to hide
Is ripping open my curtain of pride
Exposing my pain and flowing tears
That deep inside I am engrossed with fear.
To this scary darkness, I closed my eyes
Hoping that I could survive.
I surround myself with all I desire
So I won't have to face myself a liar.
It's fun for a while, and I act with strength
But the storm blows on with greater vehemence.
By its presence, I begin to feel numbed
As I live each day, it continues to overcome.
The place I must go is through this rage
Yet I remain helpless to leave my cage.

To face and heed the blowing tides
Is my release from the pain inside
I know in my heart that this is true
And is that which I must do.
Truly the only choice I have
Even though I'd been acting on my best behalf.
To not condemn myself for making stage
Is my power and my sage.
For I cannot carry on with this burden of guilt
I need my strength now to tear down what I've built.
Like the hurricane with the calm in its eye
My peace will come when I am I.

I cannot continue with my ways of before
Because it is within this calmness, I wish to soar.

Now asserting my newly found Will
The storm inside attempts to hold me back
Always threatening to block my path.
But the opposite happens as I refuse the resistance
New energy fills me as I go the distance.
I am blessed with Light inside the darkened mass
Feeling for the first time
I am living at last.

The storm is known to me as Life
All too often causing some kind of strife.
Yet with all things valuable, the lessons are tough
And one thing I learned as I dealt with my bluff.
A Power and Peace within me exists
And by accepting my pain, I was brought to this bliss.

I thought I knew it all and had it all figured out. I had created a *stage life* that looked good to those watching my show. But reality set in, and I realized I knew nothing, or very little at all. I also realized I was not a very happy person and I really didn't know what I was doing.

I was supposed to know what I was doing. After all, I was twenty-five years old. But the truth was, I didn't have a clue. Once I admitted this to myself, things began to look a little brighter, but also darker at the same time. As I allowed myself to realize that the life I had been living wasn't fun or fulfilling, some questions began to emerge: *Who am I? What am I doing here? What's it all about? Why am I not happy?*

I am on a continuous path, seeking to find a state of being, a mindset that cements me to a feeling of bliss. The bliss and the joy are sometimes elusive, but giving up is not an option. My mind is set on further excavation—removing the things that keep me from a life of joy. Like career and professional success, joy is a choice, and I'm going in!

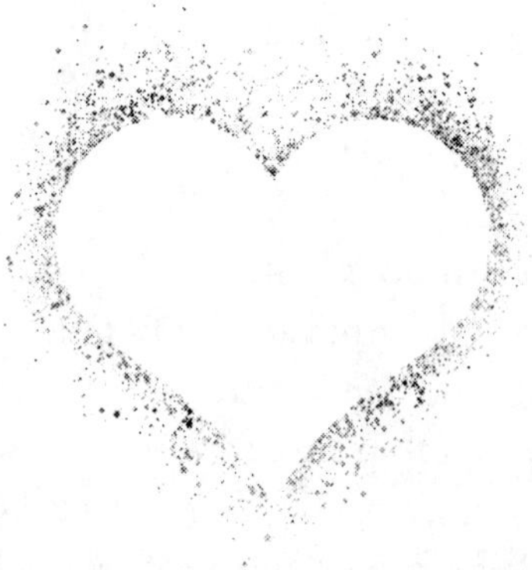

How Is It That I Can Survive?

So much heartache I have inside

Throughout my life, I have often felt that pain is a
punishment to be endured
My misfortune
An uncaring world
A hideous joke.

I do not understand my suffering.

Yet, even in my darkest moments
I want to keep experiencing all that comes to me.

Because then I know that I'm alive.

A fortune and gift that when the pain does pass
I can know the sound and feeling of a hearty laugh.
The excitement of meeting a new friend, a new love.
People caring and loving me even when I risk showing
my darkest side.
The thrill of treading new ground.
And learning throughout it all
My life is not a punishment to be endured
It's the greatest Wonder in the world.

Why would I not want to survive?

Diving Deep

I heard I was born in sin. And since sin is a bad thing, I believed there was something bad about me, that there was something wrong with me. I didn't measure up in some way. I fell for this *truth* for a long time. After all, *they* would know better than I did about what God was, what the truth was, and what I was all about. Poor, hapless human being who did not know her way. Oh, it's such a good thing that they were there to tell me. In their opinion, I was a broken, sinful creature who needed fixing—and they knew how to fix me. What would I do without *them*?

Thrive!

For it was the very undoing of that *truth* that became my path to true freedom.

The path is simple and arduous. The paradox of my greatest joy being revealed by diving into my deepest pain, is the truth of my experience.

My deepest pain was being ashamed of who I was. However, the fact is that I learned to be ashamed.

Simply Put

I was raised in a fear-based consciousness that can be summed up by an *I'm not good enough* pattern of thinking. I viewed myself in relationship to others and the world around me as *I just don't measure up*. Through competition, comparison, scarcity, the *there's not enough to go around* mentality, constantly seeing images of ideal beauty (and noticing that I don't look like that), and markers of success that I appeared not to be meeting, I told myself that I wasn't *good enough.*

Alongside societal issues, are family issues that can sometimes create and mold less than an ideal sense of self. I suppose the commonly used term is "dysfunctional," but I shall refrain from using that term because it does a disservice to the complexity of all that goes into the unintentional wounding that happens within a family. Growing up, I formed deep negative beliefs about how lovable I was due to an emotionally unavailable father. He always provided our physical needs, and many wonderful extras on top of that: figure skating lessons for over ten years (a costly sport), a trailer at the same park for fifteen years (with a boat for water skiing), and loads of other kids to play and hang with.

All of these wonderful extras were my saving grace for the emotional turmoil I went through as a result of living with this same father who could be volatile, who drank too much. I would feel great uncertainty when he drank because I didn't know if *happy dad* would show up or *mad dad.* I also heard him call me "Stupid." And at other times, he would say that I was a "Pain in the ass." There were intense arguments about money due to his fear of not having enough or being able to make enough. How confusing is that? I would have all my basic needs met—along with these wonderful extras and moments where he was very kind and loving. But at the same time, he would yell that we did not have enough money. Overall, it was very hard and confusing for my young mind to figure out whether he loved me or not, and at some point, subconsciously, I concluded that he didn't love me. I was unlovable, and it seemed there wasn't much I could do to get him to really hear or see me–that is, to love me.

My mother made her choices in response to my father. These choices were based on the beliefs she held, how she felt about herself, and what was important to her about family. She did her best to maintain the peace and keep our family together. It was often difficult for her to navigate the relationship with my father and take care of five children. As I got older, I realized I held anger toward her for not challenging my father more, and moreover, for staying with him.

I share all this to give you an understanding as to all that took place in my journey back to love—love for myself, my dad, my mom, and for being alive.

The love for myself was also challenging because I

was born with a deformed left hand. Although at my age now, it seems trivial; growing up, it was not. My middle and ring fingers are only little stubs. The index finger looks somewhat normal, but only has one knuckle, and the pinky finger again, looks normal, but is longer and bigger than my right-hand pinky. Yay for my thumb—all good!

I think we have all heard the saying, "Kids can be cruel." That was definitely the case when my left hand was seen by some. Not everyone was cruel, but the ones who were, made me feel embarrassed and made me believe that something was wrong with me. I became a master at hiding it. So much so, it would take people months to notice it as I got older. Every time I met a new man, I felt petrified for him to see my left hand and I would hide it as long as possible, hoping he would never notice. This was such an issue in my twenties; I had a two-finger prosthesis made. It was actually a time-consuming process and an expensive lesson. I didn't like it. It wasn't me. Still, I didn't voluntarily show my hand to any man I dated until I was in my late thirties. Needless to say, much healing needed to be done about this as well.

So, there was much that went into this less than ideal image I had of myself that needed to be challenged and healed. It was not an easy task. Many years of fear-based thinking and a negative self-image could not be overcome in a day, or even a decade. But it came. The Bible says, "Ask, and ye shall receive." It didn't always come in the form I wanted, well rarely, but always in the way I needed. I began a deep undoing of previously held beliefs to allow for what I was really searching for to emerge.

THE RIDE OF MY LIFE

So much to ponder, so much to decide
Life has become a roller coaster ride.
On the way up, there is hope and excitement
Reaching the top, the joy of life is heightened.
Sailing down, I experience the rush
But deep down inside, my heart is hushed.

Now the questions do begin
Can I one more time, rise and ascend?

Yet without realizing, I am swept up again
Going for the ride one more time.
Each time it is different, nothing quite the same.
Except for more knowledge of
the truth of Life's game
I must go on and never doubt
Trusting the Power within, I am never without.

Each ride to the top is a more thrilling trip
Taking away the anxiety of the upcoming dip.
Because now the Truth is very well learned
Life keeps on going, I don't take a turn.

Ride on, ride on, take the downs with the ups
Letting Life's energy flow, I will triumph.

As I got into my late teens and early twenties, this lack of self-regard, self-love, and self-value began to manifest and show up in my relationships with men. The first long-term relationship I had, was with a man who totally destroyed what little self-esteem I had.

I was with him for two years. At the age of twenty-one, he was already a father and divorcée; he was unemployed and lived with his parents. What was so appealing and interesting about him? Not a thing. But desperation does funny things to a person, and I wanted to be in a relationship so badly, I got just that—a bad relationship.

After that relationship, another aspect of myself became apparent. I was notoriously attracted to men who were not attracted to me, and I wanted nothing to do with those who were. The more unavailable he was, the more attracted I was to him. I was content enough when these men fed me crumbs of affection. It wasn't a matter of not being able to attract them to me on some level, but it was never for the *long run*, as I was always hoping and pining for. My heart constantly felt like it was being trampled on.

To put it succinctly, I was needy. I wanted them to want me. I needed to feel like I mattered. I wanted them to find me acceptable—to be approved of. Yes, I was looking for these young men to give to me the love and affection I was yearning for from my father.

As cliché as that may seem, it is what my behavior and choices were all about. The men that seemed to accept me as I was, who showed genuine interest in being in a relationship with me, I didn't feel worthy of. So, a string of unfulfilling relationships—*learning experiences* became more fuel in the fire to figure out what my life (and I) was all about.

It was during this time in my mid-twenties that I began to journal. I started this practice as a way to cope and help myself navigate a prominent relationship with a man whom I felt I was incredibly in love with. However, I did what I could to stay away when I knew he wasn't ever going to give me the relationship I thought I wanted with him. But, if he came knocking at my door, I forgot this resolution to myself and would begin the cat and mouse game with him all over again.

This vicious cycle lasted almost four years. I had other relationships in the hope that I would finally sever the bond I felt with him, but they didn't work. So, putting pen to paper began to be a way to sort out my thoughts and feelings.

Opening line of my first journal:

September 3,1986

I feel like I'm starting a new life.
I feel great.
I want to write it down, so that's what I'm doing.

Years later, I went back and gave that journal entry the below title:

MY BATTLES WITH "HIM" AND MY FIRST ATTEMPT AT BELIEVING IN MYSELF (DIDN'T WORK).

Throughout the pages of my journal, I wrote about one struggle after another—with *him*, with work, with my self-esteem, and believing in myself.

During this time as well, Shirley MacLaine's book, *Out On A Limb* was made into a two-part mini-series for television, and this sparked my memory of how much I loved that book and the inspiration that reading it a couple of years earlier had given me. I began to use the story of her journey into spirituality and her quest for answers to existential questions, as my guide.

Doing this prompted me to really be honest with myself and stop pretending that I was happy. I put on a good façade, but that's all it was—a façade. The parties and socializing were fun of course, and friends are important. However, there was an emptiness to it all. Work was fine. I had been coaching figure skating for close to nine years and decided to try a different profession. I ended up working as child and youth care worker at a treatment center in Toronto. But a few months into this new role, I realized it was not the right fit for me at all. So, one evening, in the throes of feeling both distraught with my work and relationships, and knowing I wasn't happy, I decided that this was it, *I am changing my life*. I pulled out a piece of paper, wrote down short and long-term goals with various dates in which to achieve them, and taped it to my closet door so that I would see them a few times a day.

I went back into my living room, sat on the couch and turned on the TV, feeling pleased with myself, which was when the phone rang. My life changed more than I could have ever imagined because of that phone call.

Change Comes My Way

The phone call was a coaching job opportunity in Copenhagen, Denmark.

My sister, who was also a coach, saw an ad at a competition she had been at. A club in Denmark was looking for a new head coach. She gave me the contact number, and within a week, I was sending a resume and meeting with the woman here in Toronto who was the contact person for the club there. Within three months, I was taking my first ever overseas trip to meet the club's board of directors. And then, two months later, I moved to Denmark.

By moving to Denmark, I truly brought the troublesome relationship to an end, and I was back doing work that was much more enjoyable and more aligned with my love to teach.

It was a whirlwind, and was both exciting and scary. I was so homesick the first two months, I didn't know if I would make it through the year. But one day, I climbed a tree, sat there and said, "I am here now. Make the best of it and enjoy the experience." I climbed down the tree, and I did just that. The most significant thing that happened is that I began to look at the person in the mirror. I wondered who *she* really was. Amongst everything I knew back in Canada, I didn't know who I was. Being in Denmark on my own was an opportunity for me to get to know myself.

And so began an intense inward journey. I read self-help books, journaled, joined a meditation group in downtown Copenhagen, and created a meditation practice every morning.

The most significant part of this time was what my dreams were about. I would have highly recurring dreams with two main themes. The first dream was about trying to communicate with people, either by phone or in person. I would dial a number, and I couldn't get through the call, or I couldn't get the whole number dialed before it would disconnect, no matter what I tried. And then, if I was able to speak, my mouth was full with a wad of gum so big I couldn't talk, and no matter how much gum I attempted to pull out, it would just come back to the same size wad. I was so frustrated; I couldn't speak. I was afraid in this dream because I felt like I had no control over it. I was powerless.

The second theme was, how shall I put it, very crappy. Simply put, there were not enough toilets, nor were they big enough for all that I needed to get rid of and eliminate. These dreams would occur at least twice a week and were very uncomfortable and disturbing. Thankfully, I had a friend who had some experience in dream analysis. She let me know it was a very healthy and purifying theme. I was ridding myself of a lot of psychological weight in my life. That made perfect sense. My inner work was paying off.

Then came the dream that showed me something was really happening in my psyche. It happened about nine months after I moved to Denmark. In the final scene, I was at a park in Toronto called Christie Pits, which was where my friends and I would meet on Sundays to play baseball and hang out when I lived in Toronto during my twenties. It was dark, and I was climbing up the hill to get to the road. The hill was covered with slimy, black, skinny snakes—hundreds of them. As I was trying to walk through them, they were grossing me out, and I shouted, "No, I don't like this anymore!" The moment I said this, my dream morphed and all I could see were these gigantic snakes, like pythons, intertwined with most beautiful, vibrant, and shimmering shades of purple, pink, and blue. It was spectacular, I loved it. When I woke up from the dream, right after this scene, I knew I had made the right decision to leave Toronto and was definitely beginning to blaze my own trail in life.

The coaching work was not going quite as well. In my second year there, my appendix burst and I was off work for a month. What coincided with this was a realization by both the skating club's board of directors and myself, that I was not a fit for the coaching position after all. It was mutually beneficial for me to move on. This was easy because I met and began dating a man who was a coach at another skating club in the Copenhagen area.

This started the next leg of my journey. A man who was available and whose love I could invite into my heart and life!

He lived in Sweden, taking the ferry across from Malmo, Sweden to Copenhagen, Denmark when he coached. When it was clear I would not be continuing at the club I was at, he arranged a job interview for me at a club in Lund, Sweden. Thus, I found myself moving to another country, even if it was not too far by ferry travel.

The work at this club was an absolute fit, and I coached there for five years. The inward journey was not as intense as I focused on my relationship and coaching. I felt very blessed for a long time, but there were problems and issues that kept being stirred up. I loved him, but I couldn't see myself marrying him. I would panic and feel anxious at the thought of really committing to this man. When I allowed myself to be *in the moment* and simply enjoy him and our relationship, I was happy. But this wasn't enough in the long run, and couldn't sustain us through my restlessness to change my life yet again.

One night I had another significantly lucid dream, in which I gave birth to a baby girl. My psyche was speaking to me again, and it was time to pay attention to myself in a deeper way. It's funny because after that dream, even the remnants of maternal feelings that I had about having children were now completely gone. It was clear. I was supposed to give birth to myself.

It is so interesting to me when I reflect on my life—how my soul truly seems to be the power totally in charge. As a child, I never thought, imagined, or dreamed of a wedding day—of having children. I just didn't see it, but as I grew up, the norm of getting married and having children was certainly a part of my conditioning. I began to think that this is the course in life you take. I adopted the *everybody else is doing it* mentality; if it's right for them, it's right for me. Thankfully, this path was constantly thwarted by my choice of men (and this is why it can be said, everything happens for a reason). I view these men as angels now because in truth, being single and not having children is right for me. To this day, now in my fifties, the sight of newborns and family life still do not evoke any feelings of envy or regret.

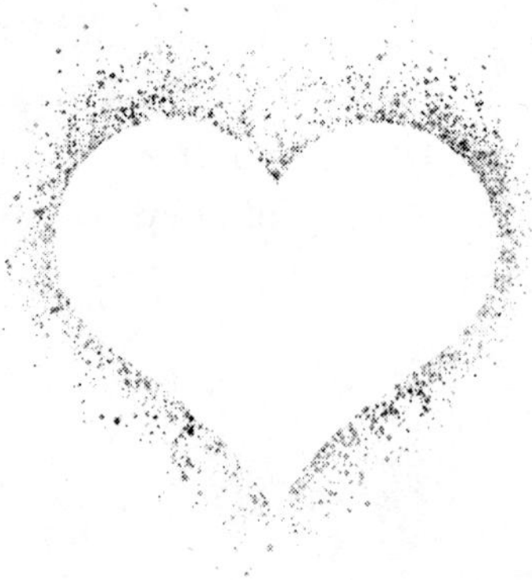

TRANSFORMATION

A mystery it was to me

All this pain and sadness I've had to endure

But through it and because of it

I have come to know myself.

And because I've come to know myself

The mystery of life has become

The Magic Of Life.

Back To Canada I Go

The relationship I had in Sweden ended two years prior, and Sweden was not my home. As lovely and beautiful it was, I missed my family and friends back in Canada. Most importantly, I wanted to go deep within myself, and I was not going to be able to do it there. It was finally time to return to Canada.

What shocked me the most after the initial honeymoon period of returning and resettling in Toronto, was realizing how much I had changed. I had culture shock! The European lifestyle was so different. I felt like I had been on a seven-year vacation. I severely missed that feeling and that lifestyle. Also, I had made a conscious choice to not plan what I would do upon my return and see what happened. Three months on welfare is what happened, as my money dwindled quickly after paying first and last month rent on an apartment, buying a cheap car, and paying for insurance, with no job lined up.

What a mess! I was miserable, but I had to keep going. I soon found work coaching again, as well as another job at a coffee shop. Not only was I completely challenged financially, but believe it or not, I met, and fell in love with a man who was totally emotionally unavailable.

A new adventure had truly begun.

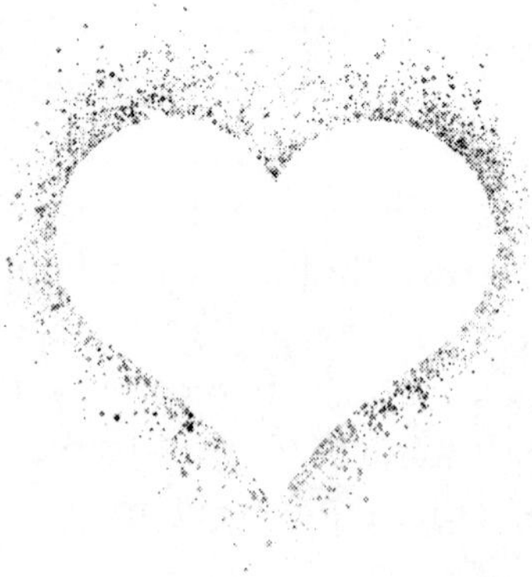

POWER

Within me

Divine Energy

Giving me strength and courage

It is mine to have

I need only allow it.

I shall not find it anywhere else

I will not find it "out there."

Trying to do so only robs me

of this treasure within.

I harness my Power.

It's God's Gift to me.

Getting What I Asked For

The layers and levels that needed to be explored were far beyond what I could've imagined when I began my commitment to finding the answers to all my questions, especially the one I had when I was eight years old, "What makes people tick?"

The relationship I now found myself in, looked very much like the one I had years earlier, before I moved to Denmark. A couple of things were different. My heart burned and yearned for this man in a way that I had never felt before. Logically, I knew to stay away and made every attempt to do just that.

But it turned out to be a journey I wasn't in control of, and logic was not going to win over my heart. I followed my heart and went into this relationship. Doing so led me to see the many distorted and unhealthy beliefs I held about myself, men, and God. The relationship between these three issues was so deeply interconnected that everything needed to be tended to for healing.

My heart shattered into a million pieces, and I cried a thousand oceans worth of tears during those seven years. No aspect was easy. And thankfully, as life would have it, what coincided with this relationship was a spiritual process with a teacher that understood what I was going through. I did have to walk the path on my own, but my teacher's wisdom helped me through some of the darkest moments.

Joseph Campbell, a writer, and lecturer wrote an essay for Comparative Mythology, titled *The Mythology Of Love* which served as a light on my path. He wrote:

> And so now, finally, what is the fifth, the highest order of love, according to this Indian series? It is passionate, illicit love. In marriage, it is declared, one is still possessed of reason. One still enjoys the goods of this world and one's place in the world, wealth, social position and the rest. Moreover, marriage in the Orient is a family-made arrangement, having nothing to do with what in the West we now think of as love. The seizure of passionate love can be, in such a context, only illicit, breaking in upon the order of one's dutiful life in virtue as a storm. And the aim of such a love can be only that of the moth in the image of Hallaj: to be annihilated in love's fire.

This was illicit for both him and I, and we did our best to stay apart. In fact, for the entire relationship, it was union and separation, over and over. A few weeks together, then back to me facing the fact that he could not give me what I wanted, followed by weeks apart. Throughout it all, I burned in the fire of love. Together or apart, I felt like I was in hell. I had to surrender to this feeling because I felt so powerless to control what I felt in my heart and soul. I turned to God in a big way, pleading for help and understanding. It was then that my anger was unleashed. My anger at God, my anger at men, my anger at the world.

One evening I allowed myself to *let it rip* in the privacy of my little home. I let loose. I yelled, I screamed, I cried. I was so angry at God for putting me through this. I was so angry at this man for putting me through this, and at all the men that trampled on my innocent heart. I was angry at my dad for not loving me the way I needed. And at the world, for not understanding what I needed. It was a purge of long held pain for feeling like I had been stomped on by such a cruel world when all I wanted to do was love and be loved.

I have no idea how long I spewed my anger, but when it came to an end, I was emotionally spent. When I realized how angry I got at God, the God that I felt in my heart and I loved with all my heart, I felt bad for being so angry. I laid down and heard a voice in my head say, "It's okay. I can take your anger. Don't be afraid of being angry at me." I slept deeply that night.

That evening was hardly the end; it was actually the beginning of me truly taking responsibility and seeing the hurt that the anger was masking. I allowed myself to feel the emotional wounds and go into them, and as it turns out, the relationship was the perfect vehicle for this. I learned to speak my truth*, even if I was clumsy. I said what I needed to, whatever the consequences were. I understood that nobody else on earth was responsible for what or how I felt. I saw how my inner child could hijack my psyche—how I would, in an instant, stop relating to others as a mature woman, and become a scared child. I was really starting to become self-aware, learning how I ticked. I didn't do it alone, but as I said, I had to do it on my own.

*As this relationship went on, the dreams of not being able to speak because of too much gum in my mouth ended.

SPIRIT

The Human Spirit

Set it free

Let it be,

A power greater than the roaring sea.

A peace in my heart that's always there

Giving it my attention I feel Life so fair.

The pain and challenges will not stop

But no more by their grip can I be caught.

To give life to this Truth is life at last

I am thankful to myself for learning from my past.

I let the present fill me with the Breath of Life

Of that which is sweetest and my birth-right

The wisdom that I Am a great Spirit

And now can walk forward free and fearless.

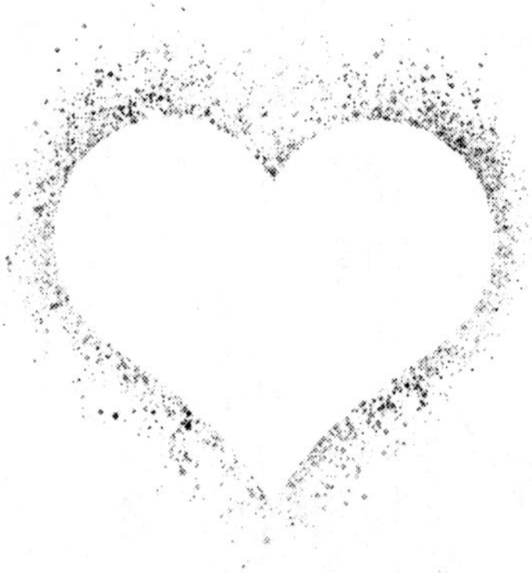

FIRE SPIRIT

The fire is burning beautifully
and the warm energy fills my heart.
My mood seems to be reflected in the flames.
The flames high and strong, reaching upwards toward
the sky, brilliant and spectacular, captivating and
powerful.
I feel this within myself; my spirit also rising to great
open sky, soaring with warmth, captivating beauty
and power so strong that it is almost too much to bear
So much all at once.

Again, it seems that when the flame dies down, so does
my spirit;
losing energy, only small remnants of the fire that
once shot upwards toward the sky in a powerful
determined dance of life remain.
I feel my soul reflected in the flames.
The fire needs sustenance to maintain its beauty
power, and purpose
just as my soul and spirit does for me to experience my
beauty, my power, and purpose.
What is my sustenance?

When once again the flames dance in front of me
I am reminded Life is a Dance.
The flames speak to me
telling me that I am a part of everything.
Just as the fire is part of the Universe
so too am I, and all of Nature.

To remember this Oneness even when the flame dies
down and the darkness comes
IS my sustenance.
I trust there will always be a spark of Life within me, a
potential flame, and dance to experience, even when the
fire in my heart fades away to a small glow,
so discreet I may almost forget it is there.
I have faith that this Universal Oneness exists, and I
am a part of It.
That I will have the courage during my darkest
moments to look for that last glow, the last spark, and
nurture my own fire and set it into power again.

Fire, Spirit and I, dancing to One Song.

How I Did It

I followed the inner calling; I believe we all get at least one. I answered my calling. I became courageous and kept following the nagging, knowing that there is a life of true peace, joy, happiness, and love to be had. I didn't stop doing this, and to this day, I don't stop because not only did I find what I was seeking, I also found that true peace, joy, and love can be forever expanded in ways I never imagined possible before. All the material comforts of the world are very nice but do not measure up to knowing true wealth and prosperity.

You name it, I probably did it. I attended workshops and lectures I found through a monthly publication dedicated to health and spirituality. I listened to radio shows that spoke about spirituality and consciousness, and read numerous books from, you guessed it, spiritual bookstores. I read books about Buddhism, Hinduism, Shamanism, Christian Mysticism, and Sufism, and embraced the aspects that brought me comfort, joy, and helped me understand what it meant to be human. I moved out of the country, thus moving away from everything I was familiar with. I had to become friends with the person staring back at me in the mirror. I meditated. I wrote at least one hundred journals, filling them with anger, pain, sadness, breakthroughs, and insights—baring my heart, soul, and truth. There was no editing, just the raw expression of tumultuous emotions and joyful moments.

Eventually, I began to follow the desire to counsel and help others with emotional and psychological struggles. I enrolled in a three-year psychotherapy counseling training program offered by the Transpersonal Therapy Centre in Toronto.

Unbeknownst to me -and it is a good thing it was- I would not only be learning and practicing to become a psychotherapist, I would have to become a client as well. That was good, very good. Diving deep became diving deeper!

I learned different psychological and therapeutic techniques such as gestalt, psychodrama, breath work, bodywork, and group process. Meditation was practiced to enhance self-awareness and the individuation journey (also known as the Hero's Journey), wherein one breaks away from tribe consciousness. My personal mental and emotional healing were a necessary component to being a person that could sincerely help another. I saw this more clearly as the first year of training concluded. Delving deep into my psyche and my shadow, facing those aspects of myself I didn't want to acknowledge but were nonetheless affecting my life experience, was not easy. But as I said, my greatest joy was being found through my greatest pain.

It was in this program that something that was buried came to light. It was having a big impact on my subconscious, and on my behavior and well-being.

Without coming to awareness of this, I am not sure where I would be today.

On one of the weekend retreats, the teacher took us through a shamanic process he called, threshold meditation. Before the process began, we were placed in groups. I shared my truth in that moment, in total vulnerability.

"It doesn't matter what I do, there is such a deep sense of sadness within me that I just cannot seem to get over," I said. The teacher looked at me and simply said, "You're ripe."

When the time came for the meditation, I was open to receiving and seeing what it was I needed. I had no preconceived ideas; rather, I wanted to trust the process. He began to beat on the drum—slowly and rhythmically, guiding us into a deeply relaxed state. Then he guided us to visualize a doorway, a threshold where there was a gathering going on beyond the threshold. He encouraged us to go in and see what was taking place. Upon "entering the room," I began to feel my muscles twitch. Then I started kicking and screaming. "Mommy, Daddy, get him off of me!" I said. I was my three-year-old self again, and I was reliving the experience of being molested. I was there, feeling him on top of me, being held down by him, and screaming at the top of my lungs, so much so, the process had to be stopped, and I needed to be *brought back* to the present by the teacher.

The interesting thing is, I couldn't scream back then, but as an adult, I let it all out. That retrieval was the beginning of the end of my deep sadness. The night terrors I had my whole life, began to dissipate. I woke a lot of people up from their slumbers screaming at the top of my lungs, as the night terrors were always the same; I was being attacked, and I was trying to get *him* off me.

After this three year program, I enrolled in a ministry course at the University of Toronto. I really felt I wanted to be a minister at the time. In that year, I learned that ministry is not a job, it is something I did with whomever I interacted with, no matter the type of work I was doing.

I took a two-year hiatus after my time at university because I decided I would practice ministry in the job I already had. I would use the skills I had gained as a result of my training, personal growth, and awareness. I continued to journal, meditate, and struggle through the relationship I was in because that, in and of itself, was one of my greatest teachers—full of great love and great heartache.

Then a call from my heart rang again. The teachers at the Transpersonal Therapy Centre had started another three-year program called, *Living Spirit*. I knew I had to do it. This was seven years after my memory retrieval in the psychotherapy training program. This program was all about continuing to heighten my self-awareness and deepen my relationship to the Divine. It was food for my soul, and I wanted to feast on it.

There were six different weekend retreats, two per year, on prominent spiritual virtues: Surrender, Forgiveness (where I was truly able to forgive the person who molested me), Essence of Self (know your own soul), The Heavenly Path (living your bliss), Godward (active surrender) and, The Fire of Love. There were breath work sessions, bi-weekly gatherings, and three six-day silent meditation retreats.

I loved every minute of it! I grew, and I gained insights and ways of being that were complete joy for me, and to this day, are instrumental in helping me live my best life.

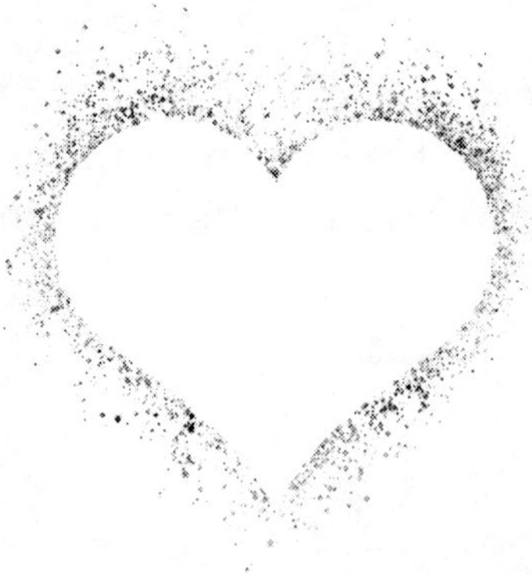

Simply Beautiful

Oh what a beautiful day today

Special it is in a simple way.

Not only the sun shining its face

But Nature's special gifts all over the place

The trees, the birds, people's smiling eyes

Fill me with a joy I cannot deny.

The song in my heart sings of pure delight

Expanding my truth of all these sights

A gift to me to love and behold

But never to abuse or call my own.

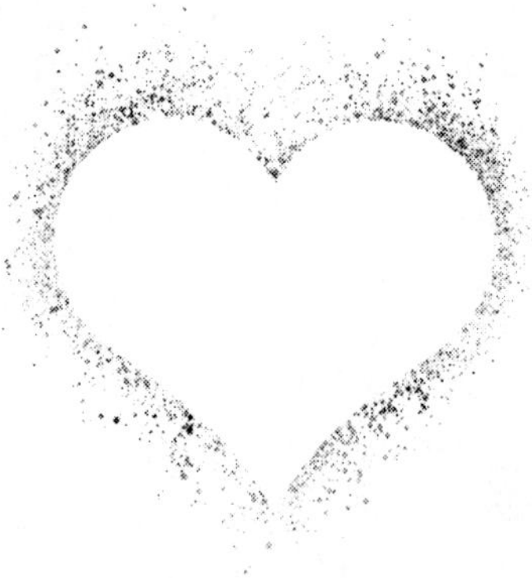

A Moment's Peace

A starry clear night
Little sparks of light.
So far up above
A sight I do love.
With these stars of the night
I on earth
We unite.
I'm filled with peace
The stress does cease.
So much power
Over me showers.
Feeling this
I experience bliss.
I am never alone
This I've been shown
As I dance with the One
Through all the seasons.

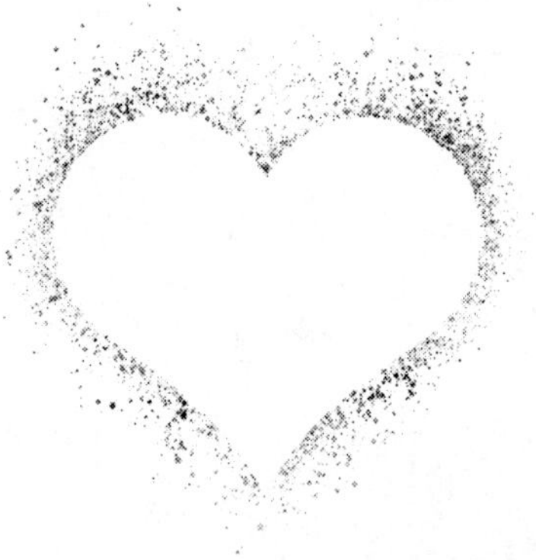

Communion

I work for God every single day,

The Mother-Father's Will guides my way.

The Divine Purpose I do express,

My reason for Being is to live like this.

From now on and forever

In each moment and hour,

I'm alive with God Love, God Will, and God Power.

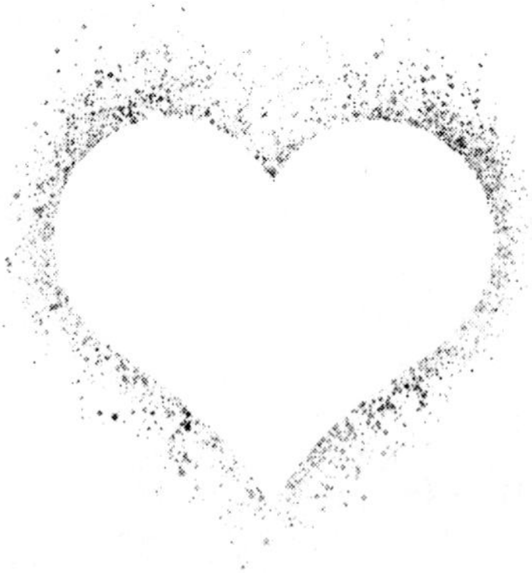

My Truth

My heart sings of new found Love

For the Great Spirit within and above.

In this Love I feel no shame

As my singing heart and God

Is one in the same.

MORE GOOD NEWS

After I had done the inner work and found a way to love instead of fear, a second awakening came my way—something I wasn't expecting.

The call came knocking at my door. It was for something totally outside of the realm of what I would normally see for myself. It was a man who had such a different viewpoint of life than mine. There was no way I saw us being compatible. Now, I'm very spiritual, no longer believing in God, but *knowing* there's a God—a supreme Love and Source, the Divine feminine and masculine, yin and yang, and consciousness beyond the five senses. He had different beliefs. All was material, physical, and within the five senses for him. He even asked me not to use the word God, as it was uncomfortable for him. I typically like to be accommodating, but I couldn't honor his request. So, it would've been easy to let him go—to tell him, "It ain't gonna happen!"

Today, this man is the love of my life. Our differing worldviews did collide for a time. But the truth is, his essence is one of kindness, and that was totally compatible with my longing; I'd wanted to meet a kind man. What he brought into my life went well beyond what I could have ever asked for.

I began to learn things about this physical world that I had no idea about; things that I had consciously disregarded because it wasn't of a psychological or spiritual realm. The central banking and money systems, geopolitics, war engineering, The Illuminati, New World Order, and false flags were new concepts for me. Negative, dark, sinister forces at work in the world—what was this man introducing into my life?

What a shock! After reading and researching further, and deciding to take the journey down this rabbit hole (something I continue to do to this very day), I am fascinated again by how much I didn't know. I began to understand the insidious nature of propaganda and how it's used as a tool to manipulate and direct human thinking. I also learned that peace could be chosen over war, and at every turn.

Jimi Hendrix was right when he said, "The world will only become civil when we choose the power of love over the love of power." These were things I hadn't been aware of before. The awakening awareness of this aspect of life is as fascinating as my inner, spiritual awakening and I highly recommend both.

Be not afraid.

And, Finally

For Now...

Being Human

I love being human.

It's the hardest thing I've ever done.

I remember being told what a human being does:

you go to school, you work, you play, you love, you have children, you help one another, you live by a golden rule.

You also listen to authority, speak only when spoken to, deny your feelings and suppress your emotions if they're not appropriate or acceptable

and you color inside the lines.

You learn what is deemed appropriate to learn and the way they want you to learn it.

You must work hard and be successful.

If you're going to do anything, do it with vigor and no thought of failure.

Failure is not good.

That edict stuck in my craw like no other.

And was the very thing that kept me from being fully human and fully alive.

Accepting myself as a failure in relationship to some idealized concept of perfection was the best thing I ever did.

Freedom was mine.

I didn't need to know it all.

I didn't need to have all the answers.

I didn't need to not be afraid, scared or vulnerable.

I was allowed to be these things

I was allowed to be afraid.

I was allowed to be vulnerable.

I was allowed to not know.

And when I was allowed these things

I took my first breath.

Inner Winner: Taking Back the Power of Self-love

My story is one of major inward transformation. I have earnestly looked into the shadow of my psyche; I had many constructs and beliefs that kept me from becoming the fullest expression of love that I could be. Some I made up from my perceptions of what those around me were doing and saying. Many were taught to me by authority figures and imposed upon me by society. So, I wonder out loud here, what if what is taught or imposed upon us is that the human being and our spirit is love, and to show it to ourself as much as to others? To speak and treat ourself as lovingly as we speak to and treat our best friend, partner or children, what would the world be like then?

One of the biggest stabs to the heart of humanity is the idea that self-love is selfishness—that self-love is narcissism, and that to put others before yourself is what it is to be a good person. I didn't grow up learning about self-love. It sounded so hokey; I used to flinch at the idea of it. The idea that conscious self-love matters at all is almost unimaginable. For me, the power of self-love is the missing link that will allow us to create a kinder, gentler, more prosperous world for all. When we have been loved and cared for by another, we feel how it helps us. Why don't we also turn it inward too and treat ourselves like we treat others?

"If compassion doesn't include yourself, it is incomplete."
Buddha

In my personal unfolding, self-love is remembering I am as important as everyone else is. It is knowing and loving myself so that I can respond with compassion and love to that which comes my way. So, I contend, if each and every one of us has positive self-regard, that is, self-love, then most of all the violence and treating each other poorly would be non-existent. I am not able to prove it, but I know when I feel love and compassion for myself, I feel it easily for my fellow human journeying on this path called life.

And most of all, I believe we will most likely stop falling for the idea that we have enemies. Sure, we are not all going to like each other, we will differ in our viewpoints and what is important to us, but there won't be an *us* and a *them*. To do no harm is natural when we don't perceive a threat. Competition would be an internal process to want to see what can be created and achieved because there's an innate desire to push oneself to the limits of our capabilities. Being an Inner Winner means *I know I am strong, powerful and creative and I can cooperate with another—I can live and let live.*

From where I stand today, I see that the disconnect—the harm and fear I have held toward others, has been manufactured anyway. I was told certain people, groups or communities were to be feared—one way or another. It's embracing being human first and labels second, if labels are really needed at all.

I think we really do unto others as we do unto ourselves. So, love yourself, and you will be quite amazed how easy it is to love all others.

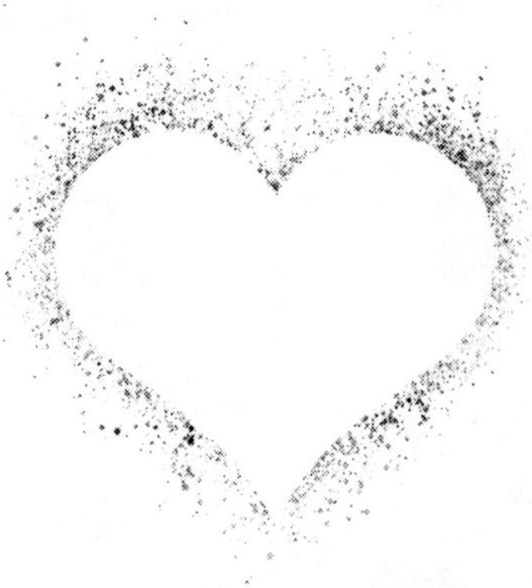

THE POWER OF LOVE

Happy are the moments I am blessed with each morn'

Love is the essence with which I am adorned.

I feel life in its fullest as it bursts from my heart

Allowing me to see light where there used to be dark.

To share this with another is a desire unbound

This power of love is ours to be found.

Allow me to give the gift to you

Then you will be giving it back to me too.

- Judy Swallow

My Counsel To You

Be courageous and follow that nagging feeling that something isn't right. No longer allow yourself to keep looking outside to fulfill the inner nigglings that keep pecking at your heart and mind. I will not lay out your journey, or tell you what you should do. Your path is unique. What is universal, however, is the calling. It may be profound, or it may just be you going to a movie that you didn't think you wanted to see. It may mean grabbing a book off the shelf that is out of the ordinary for you to read; taking up a job offer overseas or in a different part of the country; being in a relationship that isn't smooth, but you can't seem to resist it; attending a lecture or a weekend retreat. Whatever starts to show up, whatever you become aware of and feel a call to act on, do it. Trust in the unseen, the things that are felt, especially in your heart.

Also, trust that your commitment to finding peace and healing will bring to you the best people to teach, guide, and mentor you. Trauma is of varying degrees, and some suffer situations I cannot even begin to imagine. However, I know that there are skilled and loving people in the world who can help you when you are committed to becoming your best self.

Know that conscious ego will attempt to talk you out of the inner path and through the journey you'll learn why *it* sabotages. You will begin to understand why you tenaciously hold on to *stuff*, even when you know it's not good for you. Your life is at stake, and it may truly feel like a battle between your soul and ego, but it is worth being a warrior for. And by the way, as I write this, decades after beginning, the journey is continuous. Don't look for a finish line because there is no end, it just gets more exciting, thrilling and fun. And where you will travel, I assure you, you will love it.

Blessings for great love, joy, peace, harmony and a grand adventure!

Further Readings

A very limited list of the sources that helped me over the years.

Shirley MacLaine, *Out On A Limb*
P.D Ouspensky, *In Search Of The Miraculous*
Sun Bear, *The Path Of Power* and *The Medicine Wheel*
Neale Donald Walsch, *Conversations With God* (series of books)
Alice Bailey, *From Intellect To Intuition* and *The Consciousness Of The Atom*
Byron Katie, *A Thousand Words For Joy*
Deepak Chopra

The work and writings in Transpersonal Therapy:
Carl Jung
Joseph Campbell
Ken Wilbur
Stanislav Grof
Marion Woodman

Sufism:
Kabir Helminski

Buddhism:
Thich Nhat Hanh
Jack Kornfield

Consciousness:
J. Krishnamurti
David R. Hawkins
Alan Watts

ACKNOWLEDGMENTS

I want to thank Ky-Lee Hanson and her team at Golden Brick Road Publishing House for all their work and support in helping me bring this book to fruition. Because of their expertise and knowledge, they knew to encourage me to write and share more than I had initially drafted. I truly enjoyed the creative process that this entailed.

I also want to thank my teachers, Brent Mitton, Lucinda Vardey, Moira Canes, and Don Evans; all of whose wisdom was a true light on my path.

And heartfelt love and thanks to my family and friends whose presence in my life is a gift beyond words. Your love has truly helped me to grow my wings and soar to the higher experiences of joy, peace, and love that my heart desired.

To my super man, James.
Who would've thought after that first date we would be where we are today?
I wouldn't change it for anything.

About the Author

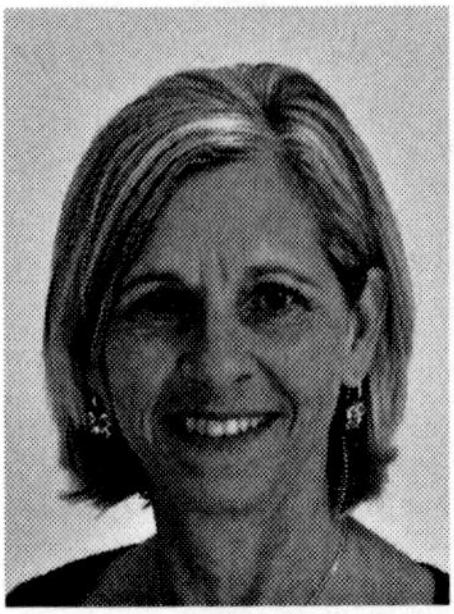

Judy Swallow is a former competitive figure skater and has been a skating coach for 35 years. She had her first real introduction to the mental aspect of sport in a workshop at a training camp in Lake Placid, NY when she was 15. It struck a cord within her and really sparked her love for psychology which soon became her passion.

As she began to pay closer attention to her inner feelings of inadequacy and the lack of belief in herself, this drove her to study and delve deeply into the subject of psychology, consciousness and mindfulness and has been doing so since her 20's.

This choice lead her step by step to cultivate a practice of self-awareness that enabled her to understand and undo all the beliefs and programming that she held within, which has taken her from feeling insecure to now claiming her presence in the world, finding her authentic voice and expressing it.